KIDS' WORK

by Meish Goldish
illustrated by Liz Conrad

Harcourt

Orlando   Boston   Dallas   Chicago   San Diego

Visit *The Learning Site!*
www.harcourtschool.com

Calling all kids! Not able to buy something you want? Don't be glum! There are ways to make the money you need. You can start your own business. Lots of kids do it!

STEP 1: Pick a Business

What kind of business should you run? Think about what you like to do and can do well. Do you like to work outdoors? You might clean yards. Do you like to work indoors? You might fix or rebuild things.

"I make money by waking people up," says Mark. "I like to get up early anyway. I make wake-up calls to people who must get up early. It's fun and easy. I don't even have to leave my home to do it!"

STEP 2: Find a Place

Now you've picked a business. Are you ready to start? You may need to find a place to work.

5

Ann says, "I walk my neighbors' dogs. I thought about the best place to do it. I chose the park. It's not far from my home. Also, the dogs can bark there and no one minds."

STEP 3: Get the Word Out

Every new business needs to be announced. You have to let people know about it.

"I rake neighbors' leaves," says Art. "I got the word out by making phone calls. I called everyone on my block."

"My friends and I wash cars," says Kim. "We made flyers. We put them on parked cars. My mom also passed out some to members of her club."

STEP 4: Gather What You Need

What will you need to run your business? Mark makes wake-up calls. All he needs is a phone. Ann walks dogs. She needs only her arms and legs.

Some businesses will need more. "I planned to sell cookies," says Tony. "I had to bake them first. I needed flour, sugar, eggs, and butter. I also needed a baking pan. My mom showed me how to make the cookies. Then I was all set to go!"

STEP 5: **Do a Good Job**

Now you're ready to open for business! Follow these work rules.

1. Know what needs to be done.
2. Do the job well.
3. Finish the work on time.

"Time is important to me," says Mark. "I can't call people late. I must wake them up on time. That's why they hire me."

"I bake my cookies carefully," says Tony. "Only cookies that taste good will sell."

STEP 6: Keep Track

Day after day, check your supplies. See how much you use each time. Make sure you have enough of everything. If your business grows, you may need more.

"On our first day, too many cars arrived," says Kim. "We had only one jar of wax. Now we keep a bar graph of how many jars we use."

Kim's Car Wash

Jars of Wax	
5	
4	
3	
2	
1	
0	week 1　week 2　week 3　week 4

15

STEP 7: Have Fun!

The best work is also fun. Have a good time in your business. Be nice to the people you deal with. Always wear a smile. Remember—a little charm can do no harm!